Mission Albania

Ten Years of Vital Christian Work
for the Albanian People

Complied from
correspondence and diaries
and the records of the
Albanian Evangelical Mission

Christian Focus Publications

Cover design: Keith Jackson

Map: Holmwood Maps and Plans,
15 Newton Park, Kirkhill, Inverness IV5 7QB

Published in 1996 by
Christian Focus Publications,
Geanies House, Fearn, Ross-shire,
IV20 1TW, Great Britain.

Printed in Great Britain by
Cox and Wyman, Cardiff Road, Reading

Contents

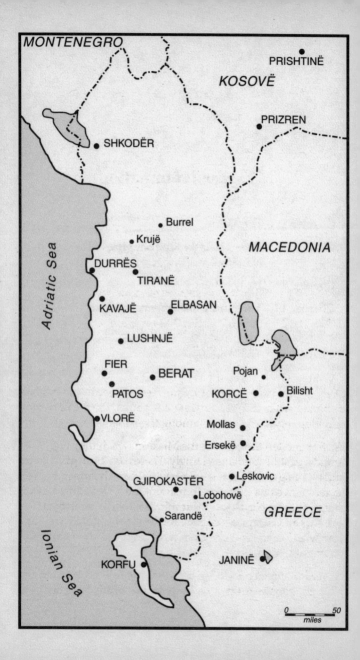

Chapter 1: Formation

The Road goes ever on and on
  Down from the door where it began.
Now far ahead the Road has gone,
  And I must follow, if I can,
Pursuing it with eager feet,
  Until it joins some larger way
Where many paths and errands meet.
  And whither then? I cannot say.

—J. R. R. Tolkien

Once upon a time there were four men, whose lives God had designed from eternity to weave together for the salvation and blessing of His people among the Albanians.

We hope to tell the story of the Mission which they felt led to found truthfully and interestingly. There have been good times and blessings, and there have been trials and heartaches, even tears. It gives us pleasure to recount God's goodness to us, and it gives us pain to turn our minds over old controversies, wounds and disappointments. As the story unfolds, we hope you will understand why we have adopted the shape and practices which characterise us today.

Albania is a place of fierce spiritual battle, and it is not the plan of this small book to by-pass the difficulties so as to present you, the reader, with a naïve, triumphalist narrative. We want you to know about the past ten—nay, twenty and more—years of our Albanian involvement, and we want you to pray with increased feeling for whatever ongoing work God may be pleased to allow us to do: to rejoice with us when we rejoice, and weep with us when we weep; so that this writing may be an instrument in forging a bond of love, understanding and commitment between us all.

* * *

In alphabetical order the four men are:

Matthew Fitter was in the police force in Guildford. In about 1984 David and Catherine Montgomery presented a profile on Albania at St. Saviour's Church, and God spoke strongly to Matthew at that meeting; from then on he had a concern in his heart for Albania.

A quarterly prayer meeting for Albania had been held since 1976 and at this time was meeting regularly in the London area. He began attending it; then, together with David Montgomery, he began a local prayer meeting in Guildford.

In the period 1985-1987 he went twice to Albania, once on the first English-speaking Christian group to visit the land, led by David Montgomery, then on a trip organised by the Revd. Dudley Powell of Stoke Gifford, Bristol.

Thus it can be seen that Matthew's interest developed first in prayer, and later in other ways, especially during the period when Albania was closed.

David Montgomery's interest grew out of a wider concern for eastern Europe. He saw an advertisement for the London prayer meeting in *Open Doors* magazine, and attended it for about a year, taking a back seat, but in time felt the Lord calling him to a more active part.

After George and Margaret Knight, who also attended the meetings, had been to Albania, David led a group of four adults and one child in 1982, on a tour arranged by Albturist. Two of the group met an Albanian girl, spoke to her about the Lord, and seemed to make an impact on her.

Alan Hall, of Open Doors, wrote and asked David to lead a larger, Open Doors group because, although Open Doors could see the need, it did not want the high profile such a tour would create. David was dubious, but agreed to do it, and found unforeseen additional benefits in a specifically Christian group. The Albanian guide observed Christian fellowship in practice; the guides became friends, and problems were less than they might otherwise have been.

So David saw the value of such trips, but he felt they should be part of the outreach of local churches. The church at Stoke Gifford became the base for future trips, and David went on three or four more, leading one because the appointed leader was denied a visa.

Sali Rahmani is an Albanian from Ferizaj in the plundered and sad province of Kosovë, Serbia.

He was born to a Moslem mother and a Communist father. To please his mother and Moslem relatives and neighbours, he celebrated all the Islamic festivals and sometimes fasted during the month of Ramadan. To please his father, he did the same thing with all Communist celebrations. But he was never converted to either of these creeds.

After finishing his studies in Economics at his home town, he worked for a year, but not being satisfied with his life he decided to emigrate to Australia via Vienna and left Ferizaj in 1972. Whilst waiting for his papers in Vienna, he happened across some Christians boldly testifying in an open air meeting, where he also saw a Bible for the first time in the Yugoslav language.

7

After a few weeks, the same Christians came to visit him and invited him to church with them. Their testimonies, lives and love attracted him more than their God. He could see people who were made new in Christ, without knowing their God himself. They were different—friendly, loving, caring, active—and he went every Sunday for about three months.

During this time, he started to understand a little of their spiritual links with God. The Yugoslavs shared the church with another congregation and the large wooden cross on the wall was a stumbling block for Sali. He could not turn his eyes to it because he was afraid that his life would be in danger as from a fetish. He said to Miško Horvatek, the pastor, "If only that cross wasn't there, I would have felt comfortable."

"We will take it away if you want," he said. "We do not worship the cross. The One who died on it is the One we worship."

He asked what was meant by sin. "Was I also a sinner? No way you can call me a sinner," he said. "I have never killed anyone, neither have I done other bad things." To be called a sinner angered him, and he demanded an explanation. As Miško read from different Bible passages, Sali felt that every verse explained a piece of the puzzle of his life. His face flushed and his heart beat faster. "How could this book know about me and my past?" It was embarrassing. He couldn't look at the pastor's face. When Miško said he too was a sinner, this made him feel better, but he felt something was wrong, for surely what man sows, he will reap. He read further, "The wages of sin is death." This was the end, thought Sali, "for sure I deserved such a wage."

But the pastor read: "*The gift of God is eternal life in Christ Jesus our Lord. For God so loved the world that he gave his only begotten Son, that whosoever believes in him should not perish but have ev-*

*erlasting life. For God sent not his Son to condemn the world, but
that the world through him might be saved."*

Sali started to think differently of God after hearing these
words. He needed Jesus and would have embraced Him immediately, but he had to think and understand how he, from
a Moslem and Communist background, could take Christ and
deny Mohammed and Communism. That meant denying his
parents and relatives. The inner struggle continued in him
for about another month.

He was grateful to God's providence for keeping him alive
over the previous twenty-two years, for he had almost died
three times. Once he wanted to hang himself, but his mother
caught him preparing the rope on one of the trees in the back
garden. Later, because he refused to marry a girl chosen by
his parents whom he had never seen, his father almost pulled
the trigger of a pistol on him as they walked down a dark
street. The third time, while he was sleeping at his relatives'
house in Skopje, he passed out for about two hours in a room
with fumes produced from an open fire. At the hospital, the
doctors were amazed that he revived.

He had never thought deeply enough about his life, or about
life's most important questions: Where did I come from?
Where am I going? What is my purpose for living?

But now he saw the cross in a completely different way, as a
great manifestation of the grace and love of God. The words
echoed, "It is finished." In a beautiful Viennese park, he felt
as if the gentle breeze of the August afternoon whispered,
"Today if you hear his voice, do not harden your hearts. For
your sins and lawless acts God will remember no more."

He read John's Gospel and went again to Miško Horvatek.
They read the Word of God again, and Miško led him into the
way of salvation. At 9:15 pm on Monday, the 14th of August

1972, in a short and simple prayer, he accepted Jesus Christ as Lord and Saviour.

His life was changed. He lost his desire to go to Australia, for it will do a man no good if he gains the whole world yet forfeits his soul. A year later, the Lord called him to full-time ministry to preach to his own people, and in the autumn of 1973 he went to Lebanon (now Northumbria) Bible College in Berwick-upon-Tweed, where he studied till 1976.

Immediately after the course, he married Helen, a Scottish fellow student, and went to Munich in association with the European Christian Mission to pioneer a Serbian and Albanian church, though of course his major personal interest was the Albanians. This work grew. In 1973 Sali had begun a radio ministry with Trans World Radio, which also grew. Literature work also began—and grew.

In 1980 Sali and Helen moved to Vienna, joined the ECM team and continued the radio ministry and evangelism among Albanians and others.

David Young's call began in 1965. He writes:

Having recently left school, I went to the town of Backnang, near Stuttgart, to work as a postman to improve my German.

There, for the first time, I met Christians from eastern Europe.

Through the church I attended, Zion Methodist, I found lodgings with the Preißler family, who had fled from eastern Germany at the end of the War. In the homes of other families linked with the church, I met elderly relatives who were allowed out on visits: being old, their possible escape was not considered too important! They were able to tell us what life was like for them under Communist rule. And I saw a film, showing the difficulties of life for a pastor's gifted son whose education was likely to come to an abrupt halt if he answered truthfully Question 7 of a questionnaire: 'What is your father's occupation?'

Some while after that visit to Germany, I saw a film made by Richard Wurmbrand, who had been imprisoned and tortured in Romania. And I heard Haralan Popov at a conference - he had been imprisoned in Bulgaria. I read God's Smuggler by the founder of Open Doors—and other books about the suffering church behind the Iron Curtain.

Time passed, and the concern and involvement grew—but how could I shoulder a burden for the whole of eastern Europe, not to mention the Soviet Union? I couldn't! So I began to ask the Lord to show me how to narrow it down, and to get really involved with one people. By now it was 1973—about the time I first met Sali Rahmani.

I had recently been sent into the ministry among the Strict Baptists, and was circulating among the churches waiting for a call to a pastorate, whilst at the same time teaching Scripture part-time in a comprehensive school. No prep was set for Scripture, so I had a good number of free periods with no marking to do, and I began to desire to use the time to learn an eastern European language. The one I felt led to would obviously be the one of the people to whom God would narrow down my burden.

I was aware that Albania was the strictest country in eastern Europe, with the worst restrictions on religion. There had been only one Evangelical church prior to the Communist take-over, and only about a hundred Evangelical believers in the whole country. I had no contact with that church, or with any individual believers in Albania, till 1990, and did not even know whether the church had survived in any form: it may have managed to continue functioning 'underground', or it may have died out. It may, of course, even have grown under persecution! Nobody knew. Yet we prayed for them.

That situation, and the sense of God's call in my heart, drew me to take up the challenge of Albania, believing that Albanian was the language God would have me learn, and that the Albanians were the people He would have me seek to work for.

* * *

In October, 1976, ten people met to pray for Albania. What a momentous prayer meeting that was! No-one foresaw what would grow out of it. The prayer meetings have already been mentioned in connection with Matthew Fitter and David Montgomery. The first was held in a cottage in Kent, called Mow Cop after the hill on the Staffordshire border where the Spirit fell on 31st May, 1807. Others were held in different homes in the south-east of England; then in a church in central London. Later, because people were travelling long distances (someone even came once from Paris!), the meeting split into regional centres round England and Wales.

It was felt that the regional prayer meetings should continue to be linked together. A prayer conference had been arranged in 1979, but few attended and the praying was largely done in glorious summer weather on the slopes of Moel-y-Gaer near Llangollen. In October, 1983, a brother from Preston arranged the second prayer conference, at Cloverley Hall in Shropshire. A conference has been held each autumn since, and people have attended from various countries and missions.

But there was still no mission specially for the Albanian people. In fact, in Britain, there never had been. Before the War there had been the Albanian Evangelical Mission, and it was a privilege and joy to have two of their American missionaries speak at the 1984 Conference, and AEM has valued its association with them over the years. Also at that conference,

David Young spoke of the need he felt for a body to be set up that would finance the work of making the situation and needs of the Albanians known to the Christian public at large especially by visits to the churches.

David visited Sali and Helen in Vienna in 1981, and from that time Sali felt interested in seeing something totally Albanian develop. Later he visited David in Wales, and—partly among the clouds on the tops of the Berwyn Mountains—they talked and prayed about the possibility of forming what ultimately came to be known as the Albanian Evangelical Mission.

In April, 1985, David visited Sali Rahmani in his new home in Hertfordshire, to discuss with him ways in which their working together could be developed. Now that Sali was back in Britain, it seemed that the time was right for closer co-operation, and they drew up a list of tasks which could be committed to David if time could be made available for them. These were mainly connected with personal follow-up of his radio listeners, and with strengthening the interest in Albania in Britain. David continues the story:

Over the next few months, I came to feel that "something must go", for a number of things I was involved with were all growing:

- *I was teaching French and German at a boarding school. This involved, as well as teaching, being on duty till 11 pm at least once a week, and perhaps four to six times a term at weekends also. Furthermore, the school was about to get a new headmaster, and he had made it plain that he was seeking even more commitment from his staff.*

- *In June 1983 a small Baptist church of ten members, two and a half miles from my home, invited me to become their pastor, and the church too was now growing.*

- *The Albanian work seemed to offer almost endless possibilities for further development, but where was the time for it?*

Something had to go, and I began testing various possibilities and trying various doors, to see which one God would open.

It was obvious to me that it would no longer be possible for the work done for school, the pastorate and Albania all to continue to grow. The time for decision came in March, 1986, when two things happened: first, I was told that our new headmaster wished to reduce language teaching in the school so much that he wanted me to work only three days a week from 1st. September; and secondly I was offered a post teaching German and French at a school in Somerset. Now the decision had to be made: was I to work as a full-time schoolteacher in Somerset? Or stay in Wrexham and work parttime? I knew that Sali had a lot of work he wanted me to do within the Albanian ministries if time could be made available for it.

By the end of 1985, other people were feeling that Britain should have an organisation whose sole aim was to work for the Lord Jesus Christ among the Albanian people—to be a focus for Christians' interest, burden and vision, and a channel for their involvement in prayer, giving and going. A number of people connected with the Albanian prayer groups contacted David to encourage him to make the extra two days available for Albanian work in cooperation with Sali. After prayer, discussion with his wife, and seeking advice, it seemed right to accept the part-time work at school and to work the rest of the time with Sali. This seemed to be the door that God was at last opening.

So it came about that, on 1st. April, 1986, the four men met in Guildford and established the Albanian Evangelical Trust (later renamed Albanian Evangelical Mission (AEM)). The Trust's two aims were:

- to make the gospel known to the Albanian people;
- to foster Evangelical church life among them.

A letter was read from Dr. Edwin Jacques, who was sent to Albania from the USA by the Conservative Baptist mission board, as a missionary from 1932 to 1940, stating his approval of the formation of the Trust and his wish to be associated with it. David Young was appointed as the Trust's secretary. Sali himself wrote one of the cheques with which the new Trust's account was opened. Almost ten years later he said, "It was my greatest joy; I am very happy still."

Chapter 2: Fiery Trials and the Shaping of the Mission

The Trust's first needs were to become known to the Christian public and to gain registration as a charity.

They had a list of about forty individuals whom they knew to be interested in the Lord's work among Albanians, and to these they wrote. Advertisements and, later, articles were sent to the Christian press, and David Young wrote to churches around Britain requesting an opening to present the needs of the Albanian people and the ministry which was being undertaken. Free leaflets were produced, outlining AET's beliefs and aims; and in September a free bi-monthly Newsletter began to be published.

It seemed that the stage was set for God's blessing and for progress in the work. But troubles were ahead, first from without, then from within—troubles which would burn certain principles so deeply into the young mission's consciousness that they would remain fundamental to its character and outlook ever after.

***

At the founders' second meeting, in June 1986, it was suggested that AET seek to hold an annual discussion with members of other missions involved in Albanian work. David Young had written to the British director of ECM sixteen days after the founding of AET expressing the hope that their Albanian section "will cooperate willingly and harmoniously with all work done for the Lord by various bodies with a concern for Albania, including, if the Lord should prosper it, the new Trust. Certainly, there is a genuine openness on our part." He was invited to attend part of the next meeting, in October, and again in September, 1987.

Nevertheless, there were two or three missions who greeted AET's formation and development with dismay, disapproval and opposition; the leader of one (AET was told) even went about telling the saints not to support them, as they were making no peculiar contribution to the work, even though they were (and still are!) the only mission dedicated solely to the Albanian people. Perhaps they felt threatened, and failed to take seriously AET's determination to pursue the aims they felt God had given them; one leader wrote to David Young that they "did not anticipate the progress that has been made during the past few months". In the interests of harmony, AET agreed to suspend advertising of the new mission for a while, so that better relationships might develop with other missions.

Two Principles

AEM's rôle is to work for Christ solely among Albanians. Over the years, their legitimate place among those who work for the spread of the Gospel in the world has been recognised. The mission cherishes its rôle, which it believes God granted to it, and when the Trust Deed was drawn up it included a clause forbidding amalgamation with any organisation unless, like AET, its only purpose is Christian work among Albanians.

Good relations with wider missions developed, and AEM hopes that an attitude of eagerness to cooperate with other truly evangelical ministries has remained and will always remain a mark of its stance.

***

For registration with the Charity Commission AET needed a minimum of two trustees. Neither David Montgomery nor Matthew Fitter wished to take on this rôle, as such a formal, public position might hinder their further visits to Albania: applications for a visa to join an Albturist package tour, the only means of entering Albania, were carefully vetted by the Albanian authorities. David Young could not be a trustee as he was employed as secretary. Sali was very willing to be appointed, but it seemed best for him not to become so formally prominent in the new society as his own ministry was being exercised via ECM and TWR. To minimise confusion and to promote harmony, it was decided he should not accept trusteeship.

David Young put forward two names, but there were misgivings among the others, who did not know them. One was Larry Quade, a friend of David's, an American Bible Baptist missionary engaged in church-planting in Wales; the other was a preacher with an acceptable pulpit manner and an ability to bring people to a profession of faith in Christ. They were willing to accept the position, and on 9th. September 1987 the four founders agreed to appoint them. From the declaration of trust in November the affairs of AET passed into their hands.

Once again, it seemed that the stage was set for progress and blessing; but in the middle of the following year, new shock waves went through the infant mission, this time not from outside opposition but from within.

Larry Quade was obliged to return to the United States for a while, and this left the affairs of the mission entirely in the hands of the other trustee, who wrote a directive to David that "you relinquish the pastorate of Llay Baptist Church by 31.8.88… or alternatively, please call to see me so that we may suspend any further activities of the Trust".

David would probably have laid down the pastorate anyway a few months later and had already informed the deacons and members of the church that both he and AET's trustees felt that it was not possible for him to exercise both the Albanian work and the pastorate; he had suggested discussion within the church with a view to an orderly transition to new leadership, perhaps early in 1989, and had in fact wondered in his own mind whether Larry Quade might be the man to approach.

The solicitor who drafted the original deed, and the one who finalised it for registration, and the Charity Commission, all stated that there was no link between AET and its employees' other activities, and that the trustees could have no authority over the pastorate. The Official Custodians department of the Charity Commission said that the trustee in question would be acting in breach of trust if activities were suspended and the Trust withered.

Nonetheless, on the 6th. July that trustee directed David to relinquish the pastorate by 31st. August. He had in fact already made an offer to the church to assume the oversight himself. And so it came about that the church secretary delivered an entirely unforeseen letter dated 1st. July to David's home, "releasing" him from the pastorate from 31st. August and stating that the trustee would take the oversight himself from the following day. David's wife received the letter in David's absence, read it, and wept. *"A good wife who can find? She is far more precious than jewels"* (Proverbs 31.10, RSV). The directive from the trustee followed a few days later.

He did get the oversight of the church, and also resigned from AET a few months later, when a further trustee was appointed in the person of Trevor Baker, pastor of Jireh Baptist Church, Pemberton, Wigan. By the end of 1989 three more trustees had been appointed: Graham Cornford, deacon of Glanrafon Evangelical Church, Llangollen, and trustee (formerly deacon) of the Strict Baptist Chapel, Mayfield, Sussex; Irvon Parry, pastor at the Independent Evangelical Church in Llandudno; and Michael Carson, deacon (later, elder) of Shrewsbury Evangelical Church.

No further trustee was added till 1995, when Larry Quade's failing health led to the appointment of David Hickman, elder at Bethany Chapel, Wallasey. It is the mission's policy that at least one trustee visits the work in Albania every year.

Two Further Principles

This trial strengthened two principles which have been fundamental to all the mission's subsequent policies.

First, it is essential that the affairs of the mission should never be in danger of subservience to one man. Therefore AEM has no single leader or director; rather, the body of trustees takes all decisions in unison.

Secondly, any member of AEM must have the recommendation of his or her local church. For it turned out that the trustee who obtained the oversight at Llay was not a member of any church, and conversations with the leadership of the church he attended could not have led to any authoritative participation by them in the matter.

***

AET emerged from these two crises chastened and considerably more cautious, and the Lord has graciously given them harmonious relationships in the years that have followed. May He grant continued peace.

Chapter 3: Early Ministry

Articles appeared by or about the Trust in various church magazines and in the Christian press: Grace, Evangelical Times, Evangelicals Now, Fellowship, Evangelism Today, Baptist Times, Christian Herald, The Connexion, Cheering Words, Christian Words, ACT Now, Voice, Redemption. David Young and Sali Rahmani spoke at meetings in England, Wales and Scotland, and Mike Brown of Swansea joined the mission as an area representative. As the work became better known among the Lord's people, churches and individuals supported AET with their favour, prayer and finance, and they were able to continue and expand the programme they felt the Lord had set before them, at home and abroad.

An area largely overlooked in Albanian ministries was Montenegro, due to the greater numbers of Albanians in Kosovë and Macedonia, and perhaps for this reason David Young had the area especially on his heart. Some 32,000 Albanians live in Montenegro, and many Albanians from Kosovë go there to the coastal town of Ulqin for their summer holiday. The Montenegrin Albanians live in and near the towns of Ulqin, Tuz and Guci, the three parts being separated by Lake Shkodër and by the Albanian border.

In all three segments, the authorities provided education through the medium of Albanian for the children of Albanian families, at both primary and secondary levels. The dialect spoken between Lake Shkodër and the coast is that of Shkodër; around Tuz and Guci there are some differences. People from some areas, including within Albania itself, find this speech hard to understand, so it is not surprising that Westerners might be daunted by the need to accustom themselves to its peculiarities; but the Lord commanded His church to preach the gospel to every creature, and Montenegro must not be overlooked.

The area is solidly Moslem, with a small Roman Catholic minority; at Zogaj the Roman Catholic church stands a few hundred yards from the Albanian border. The countryside is dotted with clean white minarets, newly built after the 1979 earthquake, and many women wear Turkish-style garb as part of the Moslem culture. People are friendly and welcoming and there are ample opportunities to talk with them. Religion plays a natural part in their lives and they feel no embarrassment about talking freely on religious matters.

A remarkable thing had happened on David's first visit to the area in 1974. Shortly before he and his wife Margaret set off in their car to visit Kosovë and Montenegro, they attended a prayer meeting in Tonbridge where a man told David that he would come to a place where he could go no further and there God would give him a vision of his future work. In Guci, Margaret had gone shopping with an American lady they met, and David went for a walk along a track that leads towards Albania: a rough, stony track. On a sudden, the strap of his sandal broke, and he could, literally, go no further. He hobbled on to the grassy bank for a time of prayer, and looking up, was deeply impressed by a striking view of the Northern Albanian Alps framed beautifully in the nearer foothills: a confirming vision of the land that God had so deeply placed in his heart.

Twelve years later, in August 1986 he spent a week in Montenegro based in Ulqin, spending the first day with Sali

Rahmani and his family who were camping nearby. Ulqin was taken by the Saracens in the 8th. century, who began its long service as a pirate stronghold. In 1571 it was captured by the Bey of Algiers, Uluz-Ali, an ally of the Turkish Sultan, and most of the influences making Ulqin what it is today have been oriental and Moslem. The market takes place alongside— and in—the main street, and there is a battered citadel high on a bluff jutting into the bay, with a ruined mosque that was once a church.

After the departure of the Rahmanis, he began visiting the area. In one village he met a Roman Catholic family and was welcomed into their home and the homes of a good number of their relatives and friends. The man had a brother who had emigrated to Canada and attended a Baptist church there. David's contact had visited the church with pleasure when visiting his brother in Canada. Christian literature and details of the Albanian broadcasts were sent to people David met.

In Tuz he was also able to chat for twenty to thirty minutes with some Albanian lorry drivers making a final stop at a café before going back into Albania.

It was a time of great poignancy. Back home, his father-in-law lay dying, and he had not seen his wife for a month. The rollicking merriment of the Germans at the hotel, singing with jovial gusto, contrasted strongly with the quietness of the deserted beach by the soft warmth of night-time, and seemed to emphasise the loneliness and distinctness of the Christian's calling to live for Christ and to make Him known in a dying world, sometimes in dark places like the nearby sorrowful land of Albania.

He spent a little time on the hillside above Lake Shkodër looking down into the forbidden land of Albania, praying, hoping, longing, wondering: would there ever be a day when the

23

Gospel and the servants of the Lord would again have access to that land?

At the end of March 1987 Sali and David set off in David's car for Germany and Belgium, to visit radio listeners and to seek possible bases for summer evangelism among the many Albanians from southern Yugoslavia living and working in western Europe, many of whom had written in response to the radio ministry. A number of homes were visited, and in some Sali and David were invited to stay and talk for a long time.

In July and August Sali and three others, including another Albanian, spent time on the proposed outreach, which included distribution of literature on the streets; personal work on the streets, at railway stations and in homes; door to door visiting; a bookstall; a visit to a refugee camp containing Albanians among others; and distribution of radio details and gospel cassettes.

In September 1987 David Young flew to Dubrovnik, hired a car and drove down to Montenegro to spend time visiting contacts again among the Albanians of that area, including listeners to Sali's radio programmes.

It was hard if not impossible to remain unnoticed. His car was moving slowly along a narrow mountain road, when a taxi approached from the other direction. As the two cars passed, the cabby leant out and said he knew him: the year before, he said, David had stayed in a certain hotel, had hired a car and visited people living locally—all of which was accurate. His visit and his identity had been discussed for no small time after his departure.

He found a heightened sense of fear, tension and suspicion, with Albanians suspected of political disloyalty, and some disappearing into prison whilst their kith and kin remained in uneasy liberty not knowing the reason for their arrest.

One day, while looking for a certain radio listener's home, David met a man in the street who pointed out the house he was looking for, and gave him Turkish coffee and cognac in his own home. Then he told him to go to the local police to register, and invited him to return to his own home to sleep overnight. However, David was tipped off that he was a *laraman*, a false friend seeking to ingratiate himself with the authorities, and was warned neither to return to his home nor to go to the police (from where it was hinted he might not return).

Another contact turned out to be a notorious informer for the police, a wicked character known even to have beaten his own mother. The address he had sent in response to the radio broadcasts was fictitious: the street did not exist, but his mail was delivered to him due to his close association with the authorities. By a providence of God, whose steadfast love always surrounds those who trust Him, the man David "happened" to ask the way to this contact's home was an upright Moslem, who invited David to his own home, sheltered him secretly for the night, and told him it was best if he quietly left the town early the next day.

David also looked for a certain Roman Catholic priest who had widely distributed *Drita e Jetës* (John's Gospel), so the Word of God was in people's homes. He was shown a worn copy in one home where he was welcomed. Sadly, the priest was away.

One contact lived a longish way outside the Albanian area, though he gave his address in Albanian. David went to an address which he took to be the Serbian equivalent, and spoke the man's name. The response was positive and friendly, though David did not speak the language of that area and was unable to understand what was really said. He gestured to inquire whether he was at home, and was told 'no'. So he asked the people to give him the new timetable of radio programmes, and a copy of *Shtëpia e lumtur*, and perhaps a Gospel or other small piece of literature. When they became aware that this was an Albanian matter, they became fearful and unfriendly, and indicated that in fact no-one of that name was known to them after all; they would not take the literature or radio times.

David was travelling with another brother, now a missionary in Tirana, and they were roughed up by the secret police in a secluded place and the car number taken. At the end of the visit, as David was about the leave the country, the security police were waiting for him at the airport, and he was subjected to a thorough search of all his luggage, repeated body scans and the confiscation of his films and tapes. No illegal literature was found on him, nor reference to the *Rruga e Paqes* (Way of Peace) radio programmes: no explanation for this treatment was given, but he was suspect within the tense, mistrustful atmosphere of Yugoslavia. His friend, who left on a different flight, was also harassed.

In April 1988 David drove to Sweden and joined Ukshin Gashi, a Kosovar believer resident in Gothenburg. They visited several places in Sweden, covering over 1200 miles within that land. Their two purposes were evangelism among some of the many Albanians living in Sweden, and to arouse Swedish Christians to the needs of Albanians.

They visited Albanians in their homes in Landskrona and Malmö, and in Hovsta they spent two days living in the same house as a Moslem Albanian family. They did door to door distribution of Gospel literature and of the radio listeners' bulletin *Rruga e Paqes*. They also used evangelistic cassette tapes and gospels.

A radio broadcast was prepared in Gothenburg for a Christian programme for Swedish listeners, bringing the needs of Albanians to their attention; private meetings were held in Hovsta and Malmö and in churches in Landskrona, Uppsala, Örebro and Linköping. Four Bible schools were visited, and David spoke on Albania at the conference of Slaviska Missionen in Örebro.

On 10th. April David was invited to preach at a church in Malmö, on the occasion of the baptism of Bardhyl, a young Albanian from a Moslem background who had recently come to Christ. The evening before the baptism David and Ukshin visited his home and had a time of prayer at which his father and other family members were present. Ukshin had a serious time in the scriptures with Bardhyl's father, and his sister Lumturie attended the baptism the following evening.

In October 1988 David and a Dutch brother called Werner, with People International, visited northern Greece.

In Feres they met an elderly man whose mother had been Albanian and his father Greek. His wife was Albanian. Two or three elderly couples were meeting together in an Evangelical chapel to maintain a witness, holding their meetings in Greek. David and Werner's host used to be an elder there, and told moving stories of Albanians he had led to the Lord, when he was working with the Bible Society.

His family left Albania for Turkey 250 years previously, and came to Greece in 1922. He himself was converted in the army after a life of sin and drunkenness. He was given a copy of John's Gospel, which he read and found interesting, but he did not know how to pray. About that time another soldier whom he knew received a letter from a friend giving his testimony to his conversion to Christ. He wrote to this friend, and received a reply explaining the way of truth. He also got books and magazines, in one of which was an article called *The Wonderful Visitor*. When he read this, there were five other soldiers in the room, so he went out to a hillside nearby, and knelt on the rocks and stones with tears, and received Christ. Thereafter he worked with the Bible Society in Katerini.

Near the Turkish border are four villages whose populations are reported to be between 50% and 100% Albanian speaking. It was said that some Albanians came during the time of Ali Pasha, some in the 15th. century as craftsmen for the mosques. However, young people now prefer to speak Greek. The Greek Evangelical Church in nearby Alexandroupolis has distributed tracts in these villages.

Most Albanians are in Tihero and trace their roots to the Vithkuq area of Albania. The village has a population of 3000, of whom 2500 are Albanian. During the 1980's they began to feel their Albanian identity more strongly, but people in high positions hid their Albanian roots.

Christian workers among the Albanians have at times attracted suspicion from the Greek authorities, and David and Werner were questioned at the police station in Tihero. It is because of past troubles between Albania and Greece that the Greek government and police are very sensitive about people who seek contact with Albanians. They fear a revival of Albanian language and culture in Greece. Also, photos were forbidden because of the nearness of the Turkish border.

Workers among Albanians have sometimes discovered distrust from Greek believers, which should not be taken personally. They may discover they are warmly welcomed and looked after; fellowship and prayer will take place; and after their departure they will be checked up on.

Fan Noli, a former prime minister and Orthodox bishop of Albania, came from one of these villages. Is it not possible that a preacher of the Gospel to the Albanian people may also be raised up from among them?

David and Werner gave several tapes away, which were eagerly requested—not because of their content, but presumably because they were in Albanian. But the Lord can speak by these means. They gave away tapes in Kipi and Feres also.

There are four Albanian villages near Florina, but no Evangelical church. They are Drossopigi, Flambouro, Ano-Idroussa and Lehovo. Flambouro has the strongest Albanian culture, and there may be as many as 3000 Albanians in Lehovo. The people moved here from the Janinë area, and here too their Albanian awareness had increased over the previous ten years.

It is best to arrive in the Albanian villages in the early evening, when people sit in the coffee houses. In the café at Drossopigi David and Werner were treated to coffee and friendly conversation, and were able to give a set of three Albanian evangelistic tapes. Also in Flambouro they gave tapes after conversation at the café.

In Florina they found two Albanian lorries by the railway station, with four drivers, of varying friendliness, but regrettably they were unable to persuade the drivers to accept a gospel tape, though they were happy to talk for some while.

Sali had sent eight addresses of radio listeners in the Albanian area of Macedonia, Yugoslavia, and David and Werner also went to visit them, entering Yugoslavia by train at Kremenica, and spending the first night in Bitola, from which town came Gjerasim Qiriazi, the Albanian evangelist who planted the church in Korçë in the 1880s. Bitola is the second major city of Macedonia, lying at the foot of Mount Perister, and its old covered market is a very small image of the one in Istanbul. The town used to number several thousand wealthy

Greeks and Jews among its citizens; it still has an Albanian minority.

David and Werner were repeatedly told that the situation in Macedonia was worse for Albanians than in Kosovë, because they are in the minority in Macedonia, but the majority in Kosovë. People were experiencing many problems with police and informers, and several Christian workers had recently experienced a month's imprisonment in southern Yugoslavia. Werner's own friends had been raided in the night by the police and literature confiscated.

Nonetheless, people seemed pleased to see them and happy to talk. The first contact was a man who in times past, had held a Bible study in his home. He had suffered constant police harrassment, and his group was scattered. No meetings were now being held, and he had withdrawn from all Christian contact. However, he was broken about this, and earnestly requested that a pastor from Serbia visit him with a view to restoring fellowship and to looking into the possibility of getting a church registered with the authorities.

They were also invited into a Albanian gypsy home, and were able to enjoy their hospitality and leave a tape.

Another call was in Tetovë, a town whose centre has been flattened to make way for ugly new buildings, but parts of it retain quaint broad streets twisting between gardens and streams. It is famous for its coloured mosque with its tiled roof and highly decorated outer walls. In this town David and Werner spent a long time talking with their contact and his brother (to whose wedding they were invited the following weekend, though time forbade them to attend). Again they left a tape.

In the Kopanica area there are Albanian villages, Macedonian ones, and ones that are mixed. The contact there was a village schoolteacher, but he was in town shopping—not at school or at home. His interest in religious matters was well-known in the village. They left a tape to be passed on to him.

In the next village, which is 100% Albanian, they followed a rough lane down to the house of the radio listener. He had had trouble from the police, who had tried to recruit him as an informer. At first he would not admit who he was, saying the man sought was out, but after conversation invited David and Werner into his home. There he checked them to make sure they carried no hidden microphones on their persons. He described how the police recruited informers, and said that 80% of his village informed. The other 20% were genuine Moslems, he said. He himself was an earnest Moslem. His son is Mohamed; his daughter has been taught the Koran by heart. He listened to Moslem cassettes and radio programmes. But David and Werner were welcome to visit him again: *Kur të vini apet, bujrum.*

The journey also took them to Prizren, in Kosovë, a town sometimes called "little Istanbul", not only because a lot of the people still speak Turkish, but also because of the many mosques. Here too was a Moslem bookshop, well stocked with tapes, magazines and books.

The last visit was to a family in Skopje, which has a population that is 40% Albanian, mainly in the outskirts and old section of the town. About a thousand of its inhabitants were killed in the 1963 earthquake, and a hundred thousand left homeless, and the town has changed much in character. It is the capital of Macedonia, a university seat, and is divided into half by the Vardar River. On one side of the bridge, possibly built in 1348, is the western, modern part of the city; on the other side, the older, eastern section. The bazaar is typical of oriental bazaars in the Balkans. It was mentioned in the Middle Ages, and is criss-crossed by picturesque streets with over a thousand shops for various crafts and trades. It is also well-known for its covered market where most of the stall holders are Albanian.

The son, who was in alone in the morning, welcomed David and Werner and asked several serious questions about the Faith. He was a law student at the University. He invited them to come back later and see his parents. His mother worked with the Albanian radio and television programmes at Skopje. His father, a manager at a factory, had Moslem parents, but practised no religion. He was more attracted to Roman Catholicism than to Protestantism, but had a lot of gospel literature in his home, including a New Testament.

* * *

From 1987 or 1988 AET had contact with a young man called Mike Brown, who had been feeling drawn of the Lord to a ministry among the Albanian people. He wrote:

> I suppose it all began during my first year at Bible College[1].
> I had had a general and prayerful interest in Eastern Europe and the USSR for quite a while, which was heightened by the particular burden the College carried in prayer for that part of the world. But gradually I found myself praying more and more for Albania, the general burden for the suffering Church being focused especially on the needs of that one country.
>
> For a while the vision dimmed, probably due to the fact that there was so little literature to read and that I didn't know anybody with a similar interest. But during my third year, the Lord brought the vision back with such force that I realised He was calling me to ministry among the Albanian people. The call was never accompanied by "thunderbolts and lightning" to make it obvious, it came via the still, small voice and an increasing burden that has never left me since.

---

[1] The Bible College of Wales, Sketty, Swansea

I began to ask the Lord to bring me into contact with people having the same call, a prayer which He has abundantly answered in the last two years. There have been many un-planned meetings and contacts which have been so obviously of the Lord.

In a remarkable way, the Lord opened the way for a minis-try trip to Yugoslavia in 1986 during which I paid my first visit to Prishtinë, Kosovë. A few months later He made it plain that He was going to take me to Albania itself, which came to pass in the form of a two-week tourist trip. Between times the Lord also gave me the privilege of doing evangelis-tic outreach among Albanians in Western Europe during which two Albanians came to Christ.

Since the Albanians are generally a Moslem people, I am preparing myself by beginning recently to work among Moslem immigrants and students in my home town, of which there are not a few. Also, I have begun to learn the language. I look forward to my next visit to Albania soon.

In January 1989, the trustees had the pleasure of writing to Mike Brown accepting his application to become AET's first missionary resident among the Albanians. The letter said:

...Underlying all this is AET's vision for seeing long-term missionaries sent to work among the Albanian people, espe-cially inside Albania when this becomes possible. The trus-tees are therefore eager to support your first year in lan-guage school at Prishtina as a step towards a future ongo-ing ministry among Albanians.

Mike's valediction was held at Mount Pleasant Baptist Church, Swansea, on 2nd. August 1989 when David Young had the privilege of preaching. On 1st. September Mike flew out to begin his ministry among the Albanians of 'Old Serbia'—the then autonomous province of Kosovë. It marked the beginning of a new chapter in the development of AET, of which more anon.

Meanwhile on the home front work continued apace. AET's first piece of literature in Albanian was published in March, 1989, a booklet of testimonies of Albanian believers for use in evangelism. It has proved to be a popular piece of writing and has generated a fair amount of correspondence from Albanians over the years.

AET was also involved with Sali Rahmani's radio ministry. David Young wrote to about a hundred and twenty of Sali's listeners and invited them to enter into correspondence further to the broadcasts, and also spent many hours translating radio scripts provided by Grace Baptist Mission and ECM into Albanian for Sali to 'polish up' and broadcast. Articles were contributed for *Rruga e Paqes*, the short magazine circulated to Sali's radio listeners.

To attract workers for current or future needs, recruitment was undertaken by means of visits to Bible colleges and the development of personal links (as with Mike Brown); lessons in Albanian were given, initially at Stoke Gifford, later at Keighley, to people interested in Albanian work; and a correspondence course and other aids to language study were produced. Booklets appeared in English to inform the Christian public about the history, religion, situation and needs of the Albanian people, and the mission pursued, and still pursues, a continued programme of visits to churches around Great Britain to promote awareness, prayer and involvement.

Giving was still not sufficient to provide for all this, and until 1989 the Secretary undertook a certain amount of supply teaching and teaching of English as a foreign language, to augment his funds.

Chapter 4: The Final Closed Years

If extreme political movements deify their leaders, it may be apt to call the two closing years of Albanian Communism a Götterdämmerung: the spiritual battle continued, and hopes grew, as Communism's day drew towards its end.

In the summer of 1989 an annual weekend of prayer and fasting began for the Albanian people. Meanwhile, the prayer meetings around Britain and the annual prayer conference continued.

Changes in Albania 1990-1991

In January 1990 Albanian premier Ramiz Alia spoke to the Communist Central Committee about a programme for the democratisation of social, legal and economic institutions to avoid the fate of other east European Communist régimes. From the beginning there was opposition from hardliners.

But those wanting liberalisation were growing restless. In January and February there were protests in Shkodër and Tirana. These were followed by arrests, but in March limited free enterprise was permitted, and the *Voice of Youth* printed an interview with writer Ismail Kadare, giving a daring and penetrating treatment of Albania's pressing issues. It marked the beginning of a new era in the Albanian press.

May saw further and more widespread unrest, in Durrës, Vlorë, Korçë, Elbasan and Shkodër, and Albania announced it wished to join the Conference on Security and Co-operation in Europe, agreeing to adopt all the 1975 Helsinki Accords. Reforms announced included:

- citizens would have the right to a passport

- religious propaganda would no longer to be a crime, though organised religious groups were not yet tolerated.

Albania received the UN secretary, marking a new openness to contact with the outside world.

By the end of May and early June ordinary Albanians were asking Christian tourists for scriptures. In June two listeners to the evangelical radio broadcasts wrote in; by the end of the year about twenty had written; three hundred by the end of 1991.

But things also had a nastier side. In July a demonstration led to the occupation of foreign embassies by some 4500 refugees—3000 of them in the West German embassy, where a large truck was used to smash through the gates. There was gunfire from the Albanian police and soldiers. And other towns experienced unrest.

The government oscillated between hardness and softness. Several hardliners were sacked, the dictator's widow Nexhmije Hoxha was removed from the Politburo, and in August Stalin's statue in Shkodër was removed. Five thousand refugees were evacuated to the West—by March 1991 the number of citizens who had left Albania reached fifty thousand. But hundreds of police and soldiers sealed off the embassy district.

In November, *The Independent* reported that five thousand Roman Catholics had attend public mass in Shkodër; *The Daily Telegraph* reported that five thousand Roman Catholics and

Moslems had re-opened a church and a mosque in Shkodër. Orthodox services were held in southern villages.

In December and January the good and bad sides of the struggle continued. On 12th. December the Democratic Party was formed; later in December fifteen thousand people attended a Democratic Party rally in Tirana. On 18th. January a crowd of up to fifteen thousand attended the first service at the Ethem Bey mosque in Tirana. In January over two hundred political prisoners were pardoned, and all remaining ones were released in March.

But unrest continued. Twelve thousand students protested about the lack of democracy and about poor living standards. In Shkodër troops and police battled with violent protesters. And there was violence in other towns, including Elbasan, Kavajë and Durrës, with 157 arrests and some high penalties of up to twenty years loss of liberty. On 3rd. February riot police intervened in a clash at a political rally of ten thousand people at Burrel. By the 16th. armed soldiers were patrolling Tirana. Two days later more than three hundred students and staff started a hunger strike to remove Hoxha's name from the University. Hundreds of police and troops surrounded the University. On the 20th. the statue of Enver Hoxha in Tirana's main square was pulled down and destroyed by angry crowds. Busts and statues of Hoxha were destroyed in Durrës and Korçë. Tanks appeared on the streets of Tirana. On the 21st. troops opened fire to disperse crowds of up to twenty thousand in Tirana. Bookshops were attacked, and huge piles of Hoxha's works burned. On the 22nd. four died in a shooting; fifty were arrested.

In March all railway stations were closed to deter the escape of further refugees. The port of Durrës was put under military control. The University was closed.

31st. March was awaited with tense anticipation, for it brought elections for the 250-seat parliament. Most towns voted the Communists out.

But town and country were split, and against the hopes of many in the West, the Communists won a two-thirds majority. The towns would not accept the results. In April the Communist headquarters in Shkodër was set on fire, and three people were killed.

Then began a twenty-day general strike by half Albania's workforce. On 4th. June the government stepped down, admitting it could no longer rule the country, and a coalition took over. It inherited a ruined land, with disease, shortages, houses and roads in disrepair, idle factories, untilled fields, beggars, hopelessness and violence.

Aid came in from the outside world, and people's desperation was such that in October thousands raided aid warehouses. In December there was looting of shops, aid warehouses and factories, and people dying in food riots. The police were ordered to shoot, and the army took over food distribution. The Prime Minister resigned; the Democratic Party left the coalition; and an interim government began grappling with the problems.

It was against this background that religious work would soon become possible again in Albania, but even as Communism was losing its hold on Albanian society, the leaders strove not to go the way of other eastern European régimes. They refused a visa for David Young when he applied in 1990 to join one of the Albturist groups; the following day he felt comforted by a word from Zechariah: *"you have been a byword... you shall be a blessing. Fear not, but let your hands be strong."* Their determination not to admit known religious workers was still apparent in early 1991, when David was again refused a visa for a tourist group.

Ministry continues from outside Albania

Edwin Jacques had entrusted the names and addresses of the remaining believers of the Korçë church to David, who began a cautious correspondence in May, 1990. It was an exciting day on 26th. June when the first letter came from the believers there. Correspondence continued, and early the following year parcels of clothes and food were sent, and also one or two Bibles; these all arrived, and there were no adverse repercussions for the saints.

From November to March of that winter AET gave an average of forty New Testaments a month to people going to Albania, plus other literature and audio tapes with Gospel messages.

New workers began to be drawn to AET. In October, David Young met Andrew Fowler, of Teignmouth, who had travelled a number of times to eastern Europe and was taking an interest in Albania. In March Kyle Tromanhauser was interviewed in Wrexham by three of the trustees. In April Paul Troon heard David Young speak at the church he attended in Stony Stratford. In June Tony Treasure, who had visited Albania a number of times as a "tourist" during the Communist years, travelled to Wrexham to meet the trustees. The Lord was drawing people together: these all joined the work full-time inside Albania in the near future.

The desire to live in the Balkans, if possible in Albania, grew in David's heart, but the Lord's mind is made known to His people and they hear His voice:

> *If you will remain in this land, then I will build you up and not pull you down.* (Jeremiah 42:10); and

> *Son of man, look with your eyes, and hear with your ears, and set your mind upon all that I shall show you, for you*

were brought here in order that I might show it to you; de-
clare all that you see to the house of Israel. (Ezekiel 40:4).

These words were applied to David's heart, confirming his
call to stay in Britain and by means of frequent visits to Albania to be able to keep the churches informed of the develop-
ing situation and ministry.

But Mike Brown was living in the Balkans, enrolled at the
Albanian university in Prishtinë. Prishtinë used to be the capital of the Serbian kings, but no traces of royal occupation survive; it is now the capital of the oppressed province of Kosovë.
There are many new buildings, and the old quarter is rather
squalid, though the town boasts a 15th. century Imperial
mosque.

It was a time of trouble, and things were not easy in Prishtinë.
Kosovë saw violence, demonstrations and deaths. Mike wrote
in February 1990: "There was much bloodshed but everything
died down when the army moved in." Three months later the
hearts of all missionaries in Prishtinë missed a few beats when
one of them, an American, was stopped at the border and his
car searched. Several letters from missionaries to the outside
world were confiscated, among them one of Mike's containing comments on the political situation. The risk of exposure
of the missionaries' true motives was greatly increased. "Some
other folk's letters," Mike adds, "were hot enough to melt lead
on and there's no way now that they don't know our activities."

Attendance at the university language and literature course
dominated much of Mike's time in Prishtinë. He passed all
relevant examinations in June 1991, and gained a fair amount
of proficiency in the Albanian language.

He attempted to "sit where they sit", seeking out Albanians,
eating and drinking with them, talking about their problems
and wishes, befriending them so as to get below the surface

of cultural friendliness to the real people. He began to learn the culture and had the privilege of making quite a number of friends.

During his second year in Prishtinë he felt that one priority was the production of a discipleship course in Albanian, which took the form of a dozen or so basic Bible studies for the new believers in the church there and was completed by October 1990. He was asked to teach the course on Sunday afternoons. Circumstances forbade the completion of the teaching, but the studies were put on to tape, making about seven hours of teaching which was used by new believers in Montenegro, Kosovë, Greece and ultimately Albania.

Mike gave a week of Bible ministry to Slovak believers in Vojvodina; paid frequent visits to Albanian friends in Montenegro for encouragement, ministry to believers and evangelism; spent time doing outreach among Albanian refugees in Greece; paid two visits to Albania; and spent a week doing practical work on the building of a new church in Skopje.

In July 1990 David flew out and joined Mike for a fortnight. Again and again there were significant and valuable personal contacts and opportunities for witness, fellowship and prayer, though it did not begin too well: the hotel receptionist in Thessalonica refused to let David into the room booked for him, and David had to wait on the street till nearly 4.30 a.m. when the receptionist came and admitted him. As the receptionist spoke no English, and David at that time spoke no Greek, no clear explanation was communicated. Neither could David and Mike enjoy the journey in a Yugoslav train, with Serbs occupying two or three seats each and refusing to allow passengers joining the train to sit down. They stood in the corridor as far as the border at Gevgelija, when Greek officials made the Serbs use only one seat each - and kept some of them waiting so long to check their papers that they missed the train when it continued on into Greece.

David and Mike joined a "Love Europe" team at Katerini on the coast of Greece and found opportunity to talk with Albanian holiday-makers from Yugoslavia who were attracted by the open-air meetings. They also joined the ECM Albanian camp at Leptokaria and enriched contacts previously made. On David and Werner's visit to Greece in 1988, it had repeatedly been said that the main centre of Albanian language and culture in Greece is the area around Thebes, where there is an Albanian choir. So Mike and David now travelled to Vagia near Thebes, which had been the centre of the awakening earlier this century, and enjoyed the hospitality and conversation of Pavlos Katërshosh, pastor of the church which was born in that awakening[2].

Visits to Albania, April-June 1991

Towards the end of 1990 it was becoming obvious that Albania would soon open up. Hence, in April 1991, Mike Brown made his first trip into Albania since 1988. There was no check on his personal luggage, no filling-in of declaration forms for customs, and only a casual check on his luggage in the coach. The border guards were friendly and relaxed.

Inside Albania Mike was able to talk to quite a few people and found that they had freedom to speak their minds regarding the political and economic situation. Some were friendly and eager to make contact with a foreigner, whilst others were more cautious, fearing it might still get them into trouble with the authorities, but all said they were currently experiencing no problems from the secret police. One was very open, and said that many of the young people were frustrated with life in Albania and wanted to leave for the West.

[2] see *The Awakenings at Korça and Vagia*, AEM, 1992

There was a great general desire among people of all ages, especially the young, to hear about God. Mike wrote, "I have never seen so many people desirous to hear the word. They know absolutely nothing about God."

Mike's main purpose was to search out the remnants of the evangelical work that had existed in Korçë. David had given him the addresses of the three elderly men who had been the core and mainstay of the small, underground fellowship during the dark years of Communism. Mike was the first expatriate to minister to them for fifty years. They made it clear that they would like to have a missionary living among them to re-start the work, and continually stressed the need for a pastor, a teacher, someone from outside to come and live there to preach, teach and send in scriptures. This was as clear a pastoral call as could be expected under the circumstances and Mike wrote, "I would suggest very forcibly that the work in Korçë take first priority above everything else."

He made a further visit at the end of May.

On 27th. June David flew from Manchester to Dubrovnik, hired a car and headed for Tuz, a mainly Albanian town in Montenegro, where he met Mike Brown. They spent two days at the home of one of the few Albanian believers in Montenegro, enjoying hospitality, rest, fellowship and prayer.

Shortly before, the Albanian authorities had expressed their willingness to allow religious workers in, and after the two days near Tuz, Mike and David joined others for the final few miles to the border at Han i Hotit. The hopes and prayers of many years had been realised, and they came to the gates of the dark land with gratitude and expectation in their souls. Thanks be to God.

Chapter 5: New Foundations in Albania

It is important to note that, whilst the Albanian Evangelical Trust was and still is the only mission aiming to bring the Gospel solely to the Albanian people, there are numerous individuals and missions which take an active and fruitful interest in Albanian ministry. These range through denominational and inter-denominational missions, young people's movements, humanitarian works and independent missionaries with various goals and methods. In concentrating mainly on the ministry of AET (later AEM), no slight is intended upon the work of others: to tell the whole story would require many hundreds of pages and of hours of research and interviews.

At the end of June 1991, a Gospel crusade was organised mainly by Dutch missions, and held in the Qemal Stafa football stadium, Tirana. Along with many others, Mike and David attended and helped with this week-long event. On the evening before the campaign proper, a vast crowd assembled in Tirana's main square and listened to a group who sang and testified. Some two thousand people attended the stadium each evening, sometimes during torrential rain; the meetings got into the national press and television; people began attending from other towns; much literature was requested; there were many serious conversations; and religion became a talking point among many interested and curious people who had been denied access to any religious literature or ministry for some years, and especially since the 1967 declaration of Albania as the world's first atheist state. The response came from a wide range of society, not least police and soldiers. In the mornings following the evening meetings, Christian workers met with smaller groups in the Park of Youth to study John's Gospel and to converse with seekers and enquirers.

The crusade finished with a mass baptism in a lake, but Mike and David saw the possibility that many of the Albanians who had professed faith had had too little instruction as to the nature of conversion and meaning of baptism. After all, most non-Moslems had a family tradition of Roman Catholicism or Eastern Orthodoxy, and were likely to expect their baptism in some magic way to wash away all actual and original sin and make them members of the body of Christ, a superstition which requires careful teaching and some time to disperse. Hence, immediately after the end of the crusade proper and before the baptising, Mike and David travelled down to Korçë, where Mike decided to live, at the home of one of the old believers of the pre-War church. They found overwhelming hospitality, more invitations than they could accept, and a great willingness in home after home to hear the scriptures and have them pray.

Korçë is a town of some 75,000 people, the administrative centre of its region and principal city of south-east Albania. Before the Second World War it was called "little Paris" and was deemed the intellectual and cultural centre of Albania. Much of this heritage can still be sensed, in the people, their values, the style of older buildings and regional music. It was the centre of the Orthodox religion in Albania. It has many orthodox and Bektashi Moslems, and the mosque of Mirahori, built in 1484 during the early period of Ottoman conquest, claims to be the oldest in the Balkans. Korçë was the only town where there was an evangelical church prior to 1991.

When Mike moved to Korçë, he was the only foreigner resident there and the first evangelical missionary since 1940. He

45

was already fairly fluent in Albanian and could minister in the language.

There were three strands to his ministry during this period:

The first concerned the appalling economic needs. There was very little food in the shops and what was available was rationed. Only cold water was available, and that too was rationed. Frequent power cuts were experienced, sometimes for days at a time. There was 70% unemployment. Anarchy reigned as a result of the breakdown of the political system, and Albania was on the brink of civil war for nine months. This all made involvement in the distribution of humanitarian aid an unavoidable necessity, and Mike played the rôle of link-man between the many agencies bringing aid into Korçë and the local authorities who helped arrange its distribution. During that first winter, distribution of aid ate up a major part of his time and energy. In those early days AET also delivered aid to a hospital in Gjirokastër, materials for a school at Gjashtë, as well as gifts to individuals known personally.

Secondly, in August he began a house Bible Study group. The first meeting had fourteen attending; the number grew quickly and soon they had to rent a larger place. This became the core of the renewed church. The pillars were the old men who had survived all those years, plus people who had been contacted through evangelism, along with Mike's personal friends. The meetings usually consisted of prayer, a few songs and then ministry of the Word. This weekly meeting led into further contacts and discussions with interested people throughout the week. Slowly, a small church began to emerge as people came to faith, and by February 1992 had a regular attendance of some seventy people.

Thirdly, the fact that there was pitifully little Christian literature available in Albanian spurred Mike to get involved in translation work. He sees Christian literature as a great support to regular ministry. So, with the help of Holger Dashi, a number of projects were initiated. This is a ministry in which AEM remains heavily involved today together with Holger and Dan Baynes.

In mid-1991, Holger was offered an Albanian New Testament by a member of one of the first YWAM outreach teams that visited the country. As a graduate in English, he expressed his preference for one in English. The young evangelist was nonplussed, explaining that the only English scriptures he had were his own Bible. When Holger got home he discovered that his mother and aunt had been reading the New Testament for some months, and their interest encouraged him in his search for God, until shortly afterwards he was called by grace to the Lord Jesus Christ.

Edwin Jacques revisited Korçë in late 1991: he first settled there in 1932 as a Baptist missionary, and remained till 1940 when wartime conditions forced his reluctant departure. After the fall of Communism, opposition to the Gospel soon developed from the Orthodox Church, and when Jacques came back they pasted posters on top of the evangelical ones, stating that Evangelicals are heretics and sons of Judas Iscariot. Nonetheless, he drew a congregation of some 240 listeners. Later, from their pulpit the Orthodox placed a curse upon the work and all who assist it.

Kyle Tromanhauser

In December 1991 AET's second missionary moved to Albania: Kyle Tromanhauser, who settled in Tirana. He sensed God's call to eastern Europe from 1981, and graduated in missiology in 1985. In 1987 he met Edwin Jacques, who put him in touch with AET. His ministry, together with his Albanian wife Matilda, consists of a secular work, bringing experts from the USA and Britain to hold seminars for the police, judiciary, businessmen and other influential people in the restructuring of shattered Albania, and in their spare time inviting to Bible studies those whom they meet from those circles and who express an interest.

Kyle writes:

> *Our ministry is one that is difficult to explain. Some of you have asked: What does all this political stuff have to do with missions? I hope you are beginning to see how Christ is using these opportunities for assisting Albania's government to bring His people into contact with Albanian leaders. It has also brought us into a unique position of presenting Biblical principles before the decision makers as the foundation of Albania's government is being laid. The day-to-day contact has given countless opportunities for a form of outreach that is foreign to many believers.*

A typical week includes meeting with Albanian staff for the purpose of growing together in the Word; a Bible study with individuals aged 23-34; and an inquirers' study composed of families from the business community; a prayer group once a week with a few judges from the Supreme Court and some staff members with the focus on Albania, the Court and those who attend.

Children's Homes

In June 1991, the trustees interviewed Tony Treasure, and his acceptance into AET as a missionary was confirmed in September.

Tony is from Surrey and was converted at the age of 19. He worked in administrative positions with various local government authorities for twenty-four years, in housing, environmental health and with the Department of Transport. He led a Christian youth group (Crusaders) for twenty years, and served as a voluntary area rep for Open Doors for five and a half years and as a Bible and literature courier, visiting Romania, Czechoslovakia, East Germany, Poland, Ukraine, Russia and China. He led the London Albania prayer group for two years. His first visit to Albania was in 1986; he paid five more visits in Communist times, and moved there in March 1992.

For many years he had felt a strong desire to do something practical in a Christian context for poor children. Albania has many large institutional orphanages, but Tony's vision was to take children into family homes managed by Christians in a caring environment with more personal attention for each child. After seeking God's direction he settled in Berat, a town on the banks of the River Osum and centre of an important agricultural region, with its medieval fortress overlooking the town, originally built in antiquity, rebuilt in the sixth century and added to in the thirteenth.

His vision is to nurture deprived children in an environment where they will have a future, and bring them under the influence of the Gospel, but things have not been easy for him. In the winter of 1993-1994, AET's newsletters contained these reports from him:

> We are regarded as rich and not always as people, more as objects which are around to give things out free of charge. Someone was murdered outside my flat shortly before I moved; I was tipped off that another group of vagabonds were discussing how to attack me and steal all the dollars which they think I walk around with.

> On return to Berat I discovered I'd joined the growing number of missionaries who'd been burgled; culprits squeezed in between the iron bars and window. More iron bars have been put up. It's unsettling, never knowing when they will try again. Certain neighbours apparently watched (and enjoyed) seeing a foreigner's home burgled, and a po-

liceman who lives at the back was on guard on behalf of the thieves. Most decent people in the district were disgusted.

Tony opened a children's home in September 1994, which he and his wife Liz are running from compassion for Albania's many destitute children, but red tape and obstruction from unsympathetic officials caused much delay and frustration.

Liz is a midwife by profession. She became interested in eastern Europe generally through Open Doors in the early 1980s and attended several prayer meetings for eastern Europe. At an Open Doors conference Brother Andrew highlighted the situation in Albania and challenged his hearers to be willing to be used by God to see the Gospel go into Albania. Liz believed God was calling her to pray specifically for Albania.

She first visited Albania in 1985 with a Christian tour group, and again in 1987 and 1989. Then she spent a year in Ceylon working with a local church in a slum shanty town area where she helped establish a small clinic. She spent several months there living in a children's home. In retrospect she sees it as a preparation for Albania.

In 1993 she knew the time was right to live in Albania, and settled in Berat because of her strong ties with Dudley and Jenny Powell who had led two of the tour groups she had been on. Also she knew Tony Treasure from the tour groups and was aware of his work towards opening a children's home.

As time went on she became more and more involved with the work for the children's home. In September 1994 the home opened and the first of the children were received from the local hospital: they had all been abandoned there, as their families were unable or unwilling to care for them. Liz began to work as matron of the home. She married Tony in Aberdeen in August 1995.

In May 1993 Mike and Judy Smith of Swansea applied to join the mission with a view to running an orphanage in Elbasan, where the Bible translator Konstantin Kristoforidhi was born in 1827.

In 1992 Judy, a headmistress, visited several schools in Albania and returned with a vision of the needs of the country, and later she and Mike both visited and met several families in their homes. During one visit they were asked to consider taking up positions as joint administrators of a privately operated children's home, and after committing the matter to the Lord they felt moved to accept. Judy took early retirement, Mike left his job as manager with a construction company, and at the age of 57 they joined AET and moved to Elbasan.

Among the first children in the orphanage were a baby whose parents were awaiting trial for murder; a boy of thirteen months whose family was in prison; a girl of seventeen months whose father had been murdered; a girl of 6 whose mother was planning to sell her for a childless couple in Greece; a boy of almost 2 whose paralysed mother had abandoned him at a hospital; and another whose mother was in a psychiatric hospital. When the second house was opened in 1995, the first two children's mother was serving a 20-year prison sentence for shooting their father.

In March 1995 AEM printed one of their reports:

> *With seventy or more clean nappies and other clothes needed each day, the unreliable or irregular water supply—sometimes on only two hours a day—gives problems of logistics. Time-wasting regulations hinder a day's work: for example, the need to take one of the babies 28 miles to his home town to prove he was alive. Sometimes you can't find the authorities because they are out drinking coffee instead of in their offices. Power cuts can last for three days, and the babies*

need to be catered for with little Camping-Gaz burners and the tops of oil heaters.

Other difficulties arise from opposition from individuals or officials who do not wish to see God's work established even in this much needed caring manner. There was even an attempt on the life of one of the Albanian staff.

They now have some two dozen children in their care.

Korçë and nearby villages

Towards the end of February 1992, Ian and Caralee Loring, workers with Open Air Campaigners, UK, paid a visit to Mike Brown. They had just arrived in Korçë, and wanted to know if they and Mike could work together. As their ministry complemented his, and because they had been previously acquainted, this seemed a natural step to take, and they formally joined AET as associate members in May 1993.

The period from February 1992 to August 1993 saw a growing diversity in the ministries of the Korçë church. The Lorings have a ministry of evangelism and discipling and this naturally complemented Mike's preaching and teaching ministry. While Mike concentrated on preaching, translation and pastoring the church, they got involved in village evangelism, including children's meetings and distribution of the Word of God among the villages surrounding Korçë, and in training the new believers as they did so.

Mike Brown was also involved as a Board member of the budding Albanian Bible Institute, which organises Biblical Education by Extension courses in some of the churches in Albania. He held this responsibility until he resigned because of a forthcoming furlough.

Soon afterwards the team was joined by Shirley Klippenstein, who transferred from ECM to AET in 1993. She had an interest in women's ministry, in which she quickly became involved in Korçë.

Shirley was born in Winnipeg and brought up on a dairy and grain farm in Randolph, Manitoba. Her parents are both believers. She was baptised at the age of 17 and became a member of the Chortitzer Mennonite Conference, to which her home church belongs, an Evangelical conference, with Anabaptist roots.

After High School, she attended Prairie Bible Institute in Three Hills, Alberta, for four years, during which time her call to missionary service became clear, although she had felt the Lord's call in that direction even when she was 13.

Following graduation from Prairie, she spent a while in secular work, until in 1983 she went to work at the Eastern Europe office of the European Christian Mission in Vienna. She travelled a lot, but was not yet aware of a call to future residence and service in any particular Eastern bloc country.

Several years later, whilst she was working at the ECM office in Northampton, the Lord made it very clear that her long-term ministry would be in church planting. As Albania and Kosovë were very much on her heart, she went on a three-month mission to work with Albanians and Yugoslavs. After the first two weeks in the Albanian camp, she knew where God wanted her, and nine months later was in Prishtinë to learn Albanian and become involved in the work.

A year later, in 1991, Albania opened, and Shirley spent nine months in Tirana, seeking the Lord for the right place and team to work in. She knew Mike Brown from their days in Old Serbia, and also Ian and Caralee Loring who at that time were in Korçë, and after several visits it was confirmed to her own heart, as well as to Mike and the Lorings, that Korçë was the place for her.

The Korçë team were also involved still in distributing material aid, but eventually this came to an end as the needs of the country slowly changed. Ian and Caralee organised the renovation of a school in Progër, one of Korçë's villages, during that summer.

Baptismal services were held at regular intervals during the summer of 1992 and annually since then.

Advance and blessing were not the only side to the story, and this was also probably the most painful and difficult time of Mike's six years on the field. Facing what is called 'mission politics' for the first time and unmasking false motives in several of the people who were attending church was an eye-opener to the reality of doing church-planting missionary work in Albania.

In July 1992, David Young visited him, and also went to Këmbëthekër, a village several miles from Korçë, where there had been aid distribution and preaching the previous month. David was invited to become the village priest! They village adheres to the Bektashi sect of Islam, and is about three quarters of an hour by foot from the point where the track becomes unsuitable for an ordinary vehicle. Work starts at 5 a.m. for the women, perhaps getting water, and the men work long hours in the fields, and chat together in the evenings on the mud path which is the village street. There are three hundred people, no shop, no doctor and no place of worship except a Bektashi *tyrbe*, a small building containing the buried remains of a holy man, perhaps some dervish or baba (or "abbot") from times gone by, where individuals or small groups come to pray or to think about matters of the soul, and outside which animals are sacrificed on the bare ground. The people seemed to want to know about the Lord. Këmbëthekër is typical of unnumbered villages in Albania. David felt unable accept their invitation to settle among them, but missionaries or Albanian workers need to live in such places and bring Christ to the villages and farms of rural Albania, where two-thirds of the population live.

Back in Korçë David felt more troubled that on any previous visit to Albania. A leader of another mission which had been involved for some while in the Korçë work, "Mr. Coppersmith" he may be called, told Mike that he and his colleagues had revelation about the future, therefore Mike should follow their advice. He put pressure on Mike to fulfil his wishes, saying that people might die and go to hell after a meeting, because Mike had not conducted the meeting in the way Mr. Coppersmith thought he ought: and their blood would be on Mike's hands. He was told that if he did not follow Coppersmith's ideas, he might well be quenching the Holy Spirit and trying to control Him.

Coppersmith has a very suave, persuasive voice, and seems to struggle against the rising tear in the pathos of his concern for souls. Enormous emotional pressure was put on Mike to bend to his wishes and presumably to allow Coppersmith and his colleagues to take over his ministry.

Towards the end of 1992 the church went through a cleansing process as they tried to apply disciplinary measures. They also decided not to work with Mr. Coppersmith's mission. Coppersmith had become linked with a small but influential group in the church who appropriated aid that came to the church for their own gain and status, and the church's amplifier and sound system. Eventually they were asked to leave the church, and another church was formed, and supported by the other mission. Mike's team found that it was then that God blessed their own church in a way which they had not known before.

There was also the time in 1994 when Mike's life was threatened. It was all to do with a 19-year-old girl who wished to go to Bible college in Athens but for whom Mike was unable to give a commendation. Her rejection by the college so angered her father and uncle that they vowed to destroy the church and threatened to murder Mike, whose landlord said, "I have never seen Mike so worried." In the night they stood in the street outside the house shouting, banging on the gate and throwing stones at the window, and returned a number of times during the day. Mike felt unsafe to venture out, and asked David Young to take his preaching engagement in Bilisht, but the father and uncle arrived and both Mike and David stayed to talk with them. However their anger grew so inordinate that the landlord was sent for and turned them out.

Plans for the next day were altered, to get Mike to a place of safety. The scheme was simple: Dan Baynes and a visiting minister from Yorkshire would take the bus to Gjirokastër, and David would take Mike in his Land-Rover to Gjirokastër as it was felt safest for Mike not to wait at the bus station. En route Mike and David would deliver literature to Ersekë and confer with a doctor anent the re-wiring of the hospital arranged by Geoff Townsend. But as so often in Albania, the plan fell apart: there was no bus; and the doctor and missionaries in Ersekë were all out.

By moving a spare wheel from inside the Land-Rover to the bonnet and rearranging the literature, it was possible to squeeze all four people in, and after a puncture on the way, they arrived safely in Gjirokastër at about 7 in the evening. After a suitable time, Mike felt able to return to Korçë; the matter died down and troubled the work no more.

In the same year this letter from someone in the congregation at Korçë appeared in the mission's Newsletter:

Beloved Brothers and Sisters in Christ,

I want to thank you for the encouragement which you have given our pastor Mike. We have received the Lord's blessings through you, David, and mainly through Mike. Mike

*began his work of building the Lord's church here in Korçë
with a few souls. Our church has grown day by day and has
reached around 170 to 200 people. Mike achieves much work
here: apart from preaching we have Bible study and teaching about prayer. And every day at his home many people
come and go, who wish to know more about the Lord. The
Lord has given Mike great spiritual power; by the Holy
Spirit, he is doing a very great work here in Korçë for the
Word of the Lord… Pray for our church, that it may grow
in faith.*

*We have gained much from this encouragement: not cars,
or villas, or wealth, but eternal life, the Lord, and salvation
from death, from the fire of hell in eternity. Pray for us and
we for you…*

Mike's team started another fellowship in a village called
Libonik, about seven miles from Korçë, consisting mainly of
young people. This is now being taught weekly by Holger
Dashi, a former teacher of English who came to Christ after
the fall of Communism. In recent months this group has seen
a big increase in numbers, mainly as a result of young people
being disillusioned with an extreme Pentecostal group which
had been working there.

Gjirokastër

In September David took a young man called Shaun
Thompson, from Mansfield, to Albania with him, and visited
Sarandë, Gjirokastër, Tirana and Berat. In Gjirokastër they were
asked to help with the follow-up of contacts made at an earlier evangelistic outreach, and Shaun had a particularly good
time. He was already seeking the Lord concerning his future,
and was aware of an Albanian calling. He felt Gjirokastër was
the town where God would have him. Two days after the visit
to Albania, he was interviewed by AET's trustees and accepted
as a long-term missionary, to settle in Gjirokastër.

Gjirokastër is the main city in south-west Albania. It lies at the foot of the Gjerë Mountain, about fifteen miles from the Greek border at Kakavi. Most of its older houses were built from 1800 to 1860, others in the seventeenth and eighteenth centuries; the larger fortified ones were the homes of the bey nobility of Turkish times. The town is overlooked by a medieval fortress captured in 1811 by Ali Pasha. Called "the city of a thousand stairs", with many of its streets cobbled, it has a characteristic charm all its own. It was also the birthplace of the Communist dictator, Enver Hoxha, who ruled Albania from 1944 till 1985.

Shaun is still leading AEM's work there.

Chapter 6: The Work Spreads

On the home front changes were afoot. It had been noticed that some people did not know what a "trust" is, and a decision was taken to change the name to Albanian Evangelical Mission. Office and literature storage needs had grown beyond the point at which the work could be run from David Young's home, and AEM's present premises were acquired near Wrexham town centre.

Literature

AEM's literature ministry continued apace. It began in 1989 with the booklet of testimonies of believing Albanians, and have now produced thirty-four different pieces of literature from small evangelistic tracts to longer writings on doctrinal, historical, devotional, apologetic and evangelistic themes. A major part of the programme is the production in Albanian of the simplified Christian classics produced in Britain by the Grace Baptists. AEM also provided translators and distribution arrangements for Dr. Sylvia Baker's *Bone of Contention*, of which five thousand copies were printed by Evangelical Press in 1995.

In December 1993, Dan Baynes of Winkfield was accepted as a full-time missionary. He was born in Tokyo to missionary parents, and after gaining a degree at Oxford and doing a postgraduate year at Reading, worked as a scientific officer at the Transport Research Laboratory in Crowthorne. He first visited Albania in July 1990, to see a Communist state before it went the way of its neighbours. He maintained contact with a family in Korçë by means of correspondence, and now lives and works there in the translation ministry together with Holger Dashi.

The use of AEM's literature in Albania by various people generated correspondence with interested readers, a ministry which was pursued from the Wrexham base.

In 1993, Andrew Fowler, Paul Troon and David Young delivered a consignment of literature to a town in the Republic of Macedonia, to a church whose pastor agreed to arrange for its onward passage to the church in Prishtinë in the plundered province of Kosovë. They also took originals of literature, for printing inside Serbia.

Geoff. Townsend

Geoff. Townsend of Neath first went to Albania early in 1992 as a result of a request from Mike Brown to his church in Swansea to fulfil certain needs. He and another member of the church went to Korçë to meet two 38-tonne lorries that had been sent and he spent two weeks helping with the distribution of aid.

He was interviewed by AET early in 1993 and was appointed to take over the British side of their aid ministry. As time went on, however, it was decided no longer to engage in general aid work, for a number of reasons: some was stolen by the authorities; it produces fake professions of faith; Albanian believers distributing it can come to feel the recipients are under obligation to them; envy is felt if distribution is accidentally uneven. In view of this, Geoff's ministry developed and changed, and it was agreed that he should engage only in specific projects in liaison with the missionaries in Albania. A major project was the re-wiring of the hospital in Ersekë. The next was to help fund an office and washroom for the Elbasan orphanage, and was completed in January 1995.

n March 1996, his work took a further step of development when he left Britain to settle in Gjirokastër and join the Mission's work there.

Ersekë and Korçë

During the early months of 1993 it was felt that the foundations had been laid sufficiently in Korçë and the team felt the freedom before the Lord to start looking to plant a church in another large town in the area. After prayer and consultation, they decided on Ersekë, about thirty miles south-west of Korçë.

Ersekë has some seven thousand inhabitants and is the main town of the Kolonja administrative district. In religion, it is about 50% nominally Orthodox, the rest being split equally between Bektashi and orthodox Moslems.

The groundwork was laid during the spring, and a campaign was organised for the month of July. As well as renovating the secondary school, they held all kinds of evangelistic meetings and forms of outreach: preaching, which drew crowds of up to three hundred; children's and youth meetings, also crowded out; women's meetings; door to door visiting; home Bible studies; hospital visiting; distribution of a New Testament to every home. The missionaries were helped by a team from California, and by some thirty-five Albanians from Korçë and Libonik. At Christmas 1993, almost six hundred people came to children's programme.

The result was the laying of the foundation for Gospel work in that town, with what is effectively a youth movement. Five missionaries became resident there, the Lorings and Shirley Klippenstein having moved, joined in July 1994 by Mark and Ruth Stoscher, together with Anxhella from the Korçë church. They have seen the beginning of a women's ministry, with regular Bible Study meetings on Fridays. However, there has as yet been no breakthrough among the adult men. The first seven converts were baptised in summer 1994, and more in 1995.

This period also saw the addition of Margaret Reid to the Korçë team. The second daughter of farm labourers who both died before she was 7, she heard and understood the gospel at the age of 32 when working as a secretary in a London bank. Soon after her conversion, she began praying for eastern Europe, which eventually led to her going to Albania. She was interviewed by AET's trustees in January 1993 and seconded to the Trust's ranks from WEC.

August 1993 saw the arrival in Korçë of the Stucky family with the American Conservative Baptist mission. They had spent the previous ten years in Brazil, doing church-planting and seminary training, and have proved a significant asset to the team and ministry of the church.

One of the Stuckys' main objectives is to regain the use of the land and buildings that belonged to the pre-War American mission in the centre of the town. Although this has not yet been realised, there remains hope that it will be possible one day. It will provide a central base for the church activities.

With the growth of the church and addition of new fellowships, the missionaries were burdened to give extra teaching and training for those that were seeking it. The Stuckys were ideally suited to this. Consequently, after they had completed a year of language study, plans were begun to start a small church-based Bible School in Korçë. This was realised in January 1995 with a first intake of some dozen students. Larry is the Dean of Studies, and seven missionaries are involved in giving teaching. Lectures are given three days a week, sometimes four, and on at least one of the other days the students are expected to be involved in some form of outreach. Larry also doubles as the senior pastor of the church in Korçë since Mike's departure for furlough in mid 1995.

This period saw the addition of the Florencio family from Brazil to the team. Manuel has been involved in church planting and seminary teaching in Brazil, and they have been involved with the Stuckys for a number of years.

In Bilisht, fifteen miles east of Korçë, there are a regular house Bible Study group and children's work, done mainly by Albanians from Korçë. In Mollas, eight miles north of Ersekë, work is being done by missionaries and Albanians from Ersekë. Pojan is the next target town for church-planting.

July 1994 outreach saw evangelism in a number of locations.

Leskovik

Also, work of an ongoing nature has been begun in Leskovik, fifty-five miles south-west of Korçë, where Joe and Rhonda Horning, Americans who arrived in October 1994, together with Andrew Fowler of AEM, are resident; Andrew was accepted into AEM as a permanent missionary at the end of 1994.

Andrew's involvement in Leskovik began with weekly visits from Korçë. On the first visit six went and were given permission to hold meetings in the Palace of Culture. They also spoke with people in the town, and Mike Brown was warmly received at the hospital. Andrew described a Moslem feast at a nearby village, with maybe two thousand people present. Each family or group of friends had brought a sheep which was taken to a building and ceremonially sacrificed to wash away sin.

Berat

The work of the children's home in Berat continued both to progress and to experience difficulties. A letter from Tony Treasure in January 1995 said:

Some officials are selfish and corrupt and don't care two hoots for the welfare of the children. I suspect that Moslems at a local and national level are out to thwart Christians' involvement with children particularly; despite the handshakes, smiles and nice words there is a lot of hypocrisy and deception around.

And by March Tony had had problems with the Ministry of Health, due to anonymous accusations that he was selling children.

He had to return to Britain for about a month in early 1995 for health reasons. Nothing was found amiss other than the stress of the work and situation, and after a rest he returned to Berat to resume leadership of the two houses he runs as children's homes.

He writes:

All hell seemed to be let loose here on 27th. December, with officials wanting to take the children back to that slum of a hospital, and demanding more documents. It's been a time of tears and downright anger. The gloves were off: this was war, naturally and spiritually for the very future of the children who have progressed wonderfully in just four months. One can tell they feel secure and loved here; their health has improved and they have put on much-needed weight. With a variety of food, warm clothing and toys Liz and I have seen them change for the better in many directions. I'm glad we don't have any silly anti-smacking (anti-Biblical) laws here - the children still hug you ten minutes later! They enjoy walks out, and the locals (with one nasty exception) have taken to them well. The nursery nurses teach them prayers, and we all sing hymns, especially during the power cuts.

We have seven staff on three shifts, two principally cooks and others nursery nurses. All do cleaning. So far all work

well and have a good relationship with each other and genu-
ine love for the children. All were unemployed.

Dudley Powell, Tony's pastor in Berat, added:

Tony and Liz are having considerable problems with docu-
mentation for the children with the Ministry of Health in
Tirana. As soon as they ask for another document and Tony
produces it, they want another! Tony is quite skilful with
bureaucracy, but it is so frustrating for him and Liz.

Later, Tony was able to write:

Dare I say things have stabilised here, and I hope we can
concentrate on running the children's home? We are now
full. Following a visit high up in a mountain village near
Tepelena we obtained the signature of a 16-year-old whose
baby was delivered following a rape by a cousin in her vil-
lage. The little girl is eight months old, and she is incredibly
beautiful.

In 1995, a Bible college student preparing for service in Albania did his placement at Berat. Afterwards he wrote:

Tony has a real gift with children. The children they look
after have been abandoned by their parents, and were being
sadly neglected in an Albanian hospital ward. While in the
hospital these children would have been left in their cots
nearly all day with very little love shown to them. They had
all been under-nourished and were in very poor health when
Tony and Liz began to take care of them, but they have been
completely changed. They are now healthy, happy and lov-
ingly stimulated children, all the staff simply adore them
and really fuss over them. All of them are very affectionate
and cute.

Gjirokastër

It was in December 1992 that Shaun Thompson moved to Gjirokastër, having spent a short while of language study in Korçë. Early in his time in Gjirokastër he gained contact with a good number of families by teaching a course in English on the Life of Christ to about sixty-five students aged 16-18 at a high school. Shaun's great strength is his warm and attractive personality, and it was not long before he had a wide circle of contacts and friends in the town. Indeed, going for a walk with him is a difficult undertaking, as so many people wish to greet him or converse with him in the streets and cafés; if you stay in his flat people visit; serious private conversation is assured only on the mountainside outside the town.

One of his contacts, now a baptised believer, worked for a local radio station, and was reading over the air the Albanian version of the simplified Jeremiah Burroughs on the rare jewel of Christian contentment, getting responses from listeners by post and phone.

In 1991 David Young spoke on the need of Albania at the church where Paul and Sally Troon were worshipping. For Paul, this talk was like an explosion; he never once dropped the subject for four months. He was then invited to go on a trip in September 1991, but he needed £500. They did not have enough money, so they prayed, and Sally's sister, who did not know they were seeking this money, gave them the exact amount. Paul went on the trip and had freedom to speak of Christ in Albania. They wrote:

> The calling in us both then really started to burn, until shortly after Sally fell pregnant [with our third child]. We tried to forget Albania.
>
> We got to the point where we could bear it no longer, so Paul approached our pastor, who greatly encouraged us to try Bible College, which we did. We were accepted on the

course, and then told about the support [which our pastor had arranged].

After Bible College we spent a year working at Cloverley Hall, where [our son] Reuben then aged 1 year 2 months was found to have cataracts on both eyes, which were operated on.

The call to Albania burned on and on! Then with much love, encouragement and prayers from our own church, we went.

They and their three sons were valedicted by their church in Whitchurch, Shropshire, in July, 1994. One of the elders wrote:

We were impressed as a church with their conviction and willingness to go to the country which had been so heavy on their hearts for so long. In June 1994 the Church recognised Paul as a Deacon and commended the family to the Mission, trusting the Lord to lead them into His harvest field, to protect them from the Evil One and to supply all their needs according to His riches in glory. They went in August 1994 leaving a big hole in our hearts and lives.

They joined Shaun in Gjirokastër, and the work built up to several home Bible studies, children's and women's meetings in Gjirokastër, and two weekly meetings in the nearby town of Libohovë. Unlike many places in Albania, however, the work in Gjirokastër is small and slow, though some have professed faith and two have been baptised in a river. The various contacts need to be brought together into the beginnings of a public church.

In 1994 David Young travelled by bus from Korçë to Gjirokastër, and happened to sit beside a man from the village of Ksamil, south of Sarandë. The journey may be fairly typical of Albanian public transport. The driver wished to refuel when he reached Leskovik, but was unable to as there was an electricity cut making the diesel pumps inoperative.

Water for the radiator was fetched from mountain streams. Of the two drivers, one had no driving licence. When another bus came the other way, the two buses stopped with the drivers' doors open beside each other so that from their seats they could chat and pass a bottle of wine to each other for a swig and a 'toast'.

Amidst all this, the passenger next to David introduced the subject of religion and bewailed the lack of any religious meetings or literature in his village. When they arrived in Gjirokastër David took him and his friend to Shaun's home and sent them on their way with a selection of literature. They invited David to visit them in their village on a future trip to Albania, an invitation which he and Shaun later gladly accepted.

To the south of Gjirokastër lies a string of Greek-speaking villages, and there are more in the Sarandë area. AEM member Penny Munden, who was teaching English in Janinë, made a number of visits to ethnically Greek villages with Greek Christian literature, but she wrote, "People generally do not realise their need of salvation." Penny's curiosity in Albania was awakened in 1973 by an article in *The Guardian*. In 1982 she learned about the London prayer meetings and also read Reona Peterson's book *Tomorrow you die*. She began attending the prayer meetings and conferences and visiting Albania and the surrounding regions. Her curiosity developed into a deep concern, and she applied for a job teaching English in Janinë. As this book goes to press, she is at Bible College preparing for service in Albania.

Sali Rahmani

Meanwhile Sali's ministry has developed and expanded.

Over the years his contacts have been invited to ten summer camps held in Greece, with a mainly evangelistic purpose. In Albania, after the opening of the land, contact was made with hundreds of radio listeners, from which have grown seven churches, in Tirana, Lushnjë, Fier, Berat, Patos, Vlorë and Seman, with a new work beginning already in Zharrës. Since 1992 there has also been an annual summer camp at Vlorë for Bible teaching for radio listeners and adherents of the churches associated with Sali's ministry. About a hundred and seventy people have been baptised at the summer camps in Greece and Albania.

A daily radio broadcast continues from Trans World Radio, and three married couples work in Albania in connection with Sali and ECM.

Krujë

The previous chapter began with the caveat that it would be impossible to give a full picture of all the work that has gone on for the Lord in Albania since June 1991, and most of what followed has outlined the ministry of people connected with AEM. To give an idea of what has gone on elsewhere too, a glance may be taken at one other work, namely that of a missionary couple sent independently from their church in Devon, who later affiliated to a Dutch mission. Why them? The fact that they were the first foreign missionaries to settle in Albania in 1991 is probably reason enough for the choice.

John and Jo Milner served for three and a half years among the Albanians of Kosovë, and managed to settle in Albania shortly before the fall of Communism—the only missionaries to do so, entering with a tour group towards the end of the Communist era, and finding accommodation there rather than returning to Prishtinë.

They settled in Krujë, the centre of a mainly agricultural region, which lies at the foot of the steep, 2000 ft castle rock. Its fortress is one of those that sprang up during the early Middle Ages, and during the 13th. century Krujë became the principal centre of the first feudal Albanian state. In the 15th. cen-

tury it became the home and capital of national hero
Scanderbeg. Nominally a vassal of the Sultan, he returned to
Albania in 1443 and began to plot for a free Albania. He seized
Krujë, united the Albanian army against the Turks, and earned
great fame for himself and for Krujë during his 25-year struggle against the Ottoman Turks. They besieged it four times; in
1450 he repelled a Turkish army which outnumbered his own
forces five to one. Resistance crumbled after his death in 1468,
and Krujë itself finally fell to Sultan Mehmet in 1478. The Turks
rebuilt the fortress, and almost nothing remains of the castle
of Scanderbeg's time.

The people of Krujë became Moslem, either by conviction or
because of the high taxes levied from non-Moslems. West of
the castle is an 18th. century teqe, a Bektashi place of worship.

In 1993 John and Jo wrote:

> Now we have come to the hardest and probably the most
> important work of all - that of seeing a church of Jesus Christ
> being established here. It is not easy to put into words all
> the difficulties the little church has passed through. The
> threats, the deaths, the fear and the bitterness in both the
> spiritual and natural realms. Some have left, some have
> joined, the numbers remain small. So often we find that the
> individuals do not make a complete cut from the dark shad-
> ows of their past lives without Christ. In spite of the many
> obstacles, the gatherings continue to take place twice a week.

> We have seen the hand of the Lord at work in so many situ-
> ations and we are very much aware that many people have
> been praying. We are now involved in ten meetings a week,
> five in the house, three in the mountain villages and two in
> a small town in the valley. During the last month or so in
> Krujë we have seen a lot of new folk coming week by week
> with a real hunger for the truth.

In 1994 they wrote:

> *The church is growing steadily. The original group of believers are growing in the Lord, and are at last beginning to learn to work together. We have started a prayer meeting every Sunday evening which has proved to be a time of much blessing, and the presence of the Lord has been known in our midst. Also we have started having a communion service once a month. We rejoice over souls who, in the last few months, have been born into the Kingdom of God in Krujë and there are quite a handful of folk who are seriously seeking God and coming regularly to the meetings. We are aware that the work of building a strong church of Jesus Christ is going to be a long hard task.*

By November 1995 the Lord was answering John and Jo's hearts' cry to Him for the Krujë area. Believers were doing some heart-searching concerning their real motives; some who had been lukewarm were facing the decision to be "hot" or "cold", for the presence of lukewarm believers in meetings was felt to be a hindrance to others who really wanted God. Numbers had increased in the young people's meetings, and the meetings for older youngsters were more worshipful and less 'club-like': several also asked to come to the adult meetings.

Where husbands or parents did not permit believers to attend the meetings, John and Jo visited their homes and, where possible, had regular Bible studies and prayer.

Many people in Krujë believe that faith in Jesus Christ is the true way to Heaven, but are not yet prepared openly to confess Him.

Chapter 7: A New Phase

The first ten years of the Mission's life are now drawing to a close. Some, maybe all, have a dawning sense that a new phase in the life and development of the work is beginning, with things to cause concern, and others to excite and challenge.

The generation of believers brought to Christ in the awakening of the late 1930's has almost passed. Among them, Ligor Çina, elder of the church in Korçë, was a faithful follower of the Lord all through the ensuing years. His death took place on 19th. February 1995 in Korçë hospital where he had been taken the previous week with water on his lungs and a deteriorating heart condition. The funeral took place at the Korçë cemetery the following day. He was 74.

Mike Brown visited him for the last time a few days before. He was witnessing to his faith to those around him. Those who were with him when he died said that he was up and praying with them. He got back into bed to lie down, when suddenly the Lord took him. There was no suffering. He witnessed, prayed and lived his faith to the last.

His desire had always been that *Ç'mik na është Jezu Krishti* (What a Friend we have in Jesus) be sung at his funeral. It was sung at the close of the service, and was a strong witness to the family of the comfort that Christ gives and of the living power of the Gospel.

Albania no longer exercises the charm of novelty among the British public. When the land opened up in 1991, Britain's national media gave massive coverage to the plight found in Europe's poorest country. Christians and non-Christians saw the television reports, heard the wireless and read the newspapers, and sent money pouring into AET's work, a lot of it designated for the taking of humanitarian aid. But now one hears little of Albania, and some of the Lord's people are writing in to say they no longer wish to take an interest in Albania as their attention has been drawn elsewhere.

In Albania itself, for some time after the fall of Communism, there was widespread, acute hunger for religious conversation, literature and meetings: everyone wanted to know about God! It seemed that any religious "tom, dick or harry" could gain a congregation for his ideas, and among those who went, trained and untrained, experienced and inexperienced, teams and independents, were men and women who made known the true and only Gospel of the Lord Jesus Christ. Hearers gathered, people believed, and congregations quickly sprang up. This is no longer the case. True, it is easier to gain a hearing than it is in Britain, and if success in church-planting were a man's goal he would be more likely to achieve it in Albania than in Britain; but the trend of interest is indubitably downwards, as people grapple with the hard realities of living in what remains Europe's poorest country. It is neither accurate nor gracious merely to dismiss them as sliding into creeping materialism: with a reputed 70% unemployment, tiny welfare benefits, and a widespread and chronic wave of crime and corruption, they simply have to turn their minds to the demanding task of survival for themselves and their families. For many this means an arduous and long walk over the Grammoz mountains without a visa, to find illegal casual labour in Greece where a waiter may earn more in a day than a headmaster in Albania in a month.

Here is a letter from Shkodër in the north of Albania from one such refugee:

> I left for Greece as a refugee together with two brothers and two friends. We travelled for a whole week through the Greek mountains, day and night, until even our food ran out. At 9.45 pm the Greek police caught me. My brothers and friends got away, but I was put into prison in Janinë. I was kept there two nights and a day; they took all the little money we had, both Greek drachmas and Albanian leks. They put us into a bus and took us back to the Albanian border. My brothers remained there in the Greek mountains to get food, and from the night when we were separated we have heard nothing from them.

These people should not be condemned as materialists who forget God. Their need is desperate and urgent. They need Christ, but are more acutely aware that they need the means to survive these dire days.

In the winter of 1995-6 Margaret Reid wrote: "Things are changing. When religious freedom came in 1991 there was a tremendous openness to the gospel, but sadly that is no longer the case and most people are searching only for material gain. It seems that a hardness has come upon people and they're too busy to listen." Ian Loring wrote, "It has been our hardest year yet."

Ian discovered that it was becoming increasingly difficult to rent a government building for church activities, and he became more and more aware of the need to purchase a building. The Ersekë church prayed and, with American financial backing, was able to purchase a suitable building complete with 1200 sq. metres of land. This is now being refurbished and will be fitted out as a chapel for the church's use.

The Mission's January 1996 Newsletter reported that the police had recently called Ian in, to inquire into allegations that the chapel was to be used as a spy centre, or as a centre from which to smuggle girls into Greece for prostitution.

If the attitude of officialdom becomes less favourable towards evangelical meetings, it may become necessary for more and more Albanian churches to find alternative arrangements for meeting together.

Towards the end of the first five open years in Albania, a number of AEM's workers were obliged to leave the field. Shirley Klippenstein developed kidney failure, and in mid 1995 had to return home to Canada. Mike Brown, on the field since 1989, felt a desperate need for rest and a "recharging of his batteries", and left for a sabbatical year of further studies at theological seminary. The Troons' youngest son developed leukaemia, and they were obliged to return to Britain towards the close of 1995 for him to have two years of treatment at Manchester Children's Hospital. These were good people, all of them, and their departure has left a huge gap.

Albania needs long-term commitment from the Lord's people, both those who go, and those who undertake to support them. There are more young people per head of the population than anywhere else in Europe, and the majority of those turning to Christ are in their teens and twenties. It will take years for them to grow both humanly and in Christ, to marry, bring up children and establish Christian households and mature churches all over Albania. It is not a time to say our attention is now being drawn elsewhere: it is a time to take stock, to see the young, emerging churches, and to pledge ourselves in the sight of God to pray, give and work for many decades to come to see a permanent true witness to the Lord Jesus Christ established throughout the land.

It is time also to reach out to the million Albanians in the neighbouring Republic of Macedonia, and bring the news of eternal life through Christ to them, and never to forget Serbian province of Kosovë and its neighbour Montenegro, with their two million indigenous Albanians.

It is time to recruit and send our best: men and women with a deep, serious call and clear vision to undertake evangelism and Bible teaching among those who once made up Europe's only predominantly Moslem country, then the world's first atheist state. Albania calls; if God calls you too, it is time to act.

Epilogue

*'What a tale we have been in, Mr. Frodo, haven't we?' he
said. 'I wish I could hear it told!... I wish I could hear it!
And I wonder how it will go on after our part.'*

J. R. R. Tolkien, *The Lord of the Rings*

The Mission's address is:

Albanian Evangelical Mission
29 Bridge Street
Penybryn
Wrexham
LL13 7HP